A LIFEBUILDER BIBLE STUDY

J O H N

The Way to True Life

26 Studies in 2 Parts
for individuals or groups

Douglas Connelly

With Notes for Leaders

SCRIPTURE UNION
130 City Road, London EC1V 2NJ

To Jon

© *1990 by Douglas Connelly*
First published in the United States by InterVarsity Press
First published in Great Britain by Scripture Union, 1992

All Scripture quotations, unless otherwise indicated, are taken from the Holy Bible, New International Version. Copyright © *1973, 1978, 1984 by International Bible Society, published by Hodder and Stoughton.*

Cover photograph: Robert Flesher

ISBN 0 86201 779 3

Printed in England by Ebenezer Baylis & Son Limited, The Trinity Press, Worcester and London

Contents

Getting the Most
from LifeBuilder Bible Studies

Many of us long to fill our minds and our lives with Scripture. We desire to be transformed by its message. LifeBuilder Bible Studies are designed to be an exciting and challenging way to do just that. They help us to be guided by God's Word in every area of life.

How They Work

LifeBuilder Bible Studies have a number of distinctive features. Perhaps the most important is that they are *inductive* rather than *deductive*. In other words, they lead us to *discover* what the Bible says rather than simply *telling* us what it says.

They are also thought provoking. They help us to think about the meaning of the passage so that we can truly understand what the author is saying. The questions require more than one-word answers.

The studies are personal. Questions expose us to the promises, assurances, exhortations and challenges of God's Word. They are designed to allow the Scriptures to renew our minds so that we can be transformed by the Spirit of God. This is the ultimate goal of all Bible study.

The studies are versatile. They are designed for student, neighborhood and church groups. They are also effective for individual study.

How They're Put Together

LifeBuilder Bible Studies also have a distinctive format. Each study need take no more than forty-five minutes in a group setting or thirty minutes in personal study – unless you choose to take more time.

The studies can be used within a quarter system in a church and fit well in a semester or trimester system on a college campus. If a guide has more than thirteen studies, it is divided into two or occasionally three parts of approximately twelve studies each.

LifeBuilder Bible Studies use a workbook format. Space is provided for writing answers to each question. This is ideal for personal study and allows group members to prepare in advance for the discussion.

The studies also contain leader's notes. They show how to lead a group discussion, provide additional background information on certain questions, give helpful tips on group dynamics and suggest ways to deal with problems which may arise during the discussion. With such helps, someone with little or no experience can lead an effective study.

Suggestions for Individual Study

1. As you begin each study, pray that God will help you to understand and apply the passage to your life.

2. Read and reread the assigned Bible passage to familiarize yourself with what the author is saying. In the case of book studies, you may want to read through the entire book prior to the first study. This will give you a helpful overview of its contents.

3. A good modern translation of the Bible, rather than the King James Version or a paraphrase, will give you the most help. The New International Version, the New American Standard Bible and the Revised Standard Version are all recommended. However, the questions in this guide are based on the New International Version.

4. Write your answers in the space provided in the study guide. This will help you to express your understanding of the passage clearly.

5. It might be good to have a Bible dictionary handy. Use it to look up any unfamiliar words, names or places.

Suggestions for Group Study

1. Come to the study prepared. Follow the suggestions for individual study mentioned above. You will find that careful preparation will greatly enrich your time spent in group discussion.

2. Be willing to participate in the discussion. The leader of your group will not be lecturing. Instead, he or she will be encouraging the members of the group to discuss what they have learned from the passage. The leader will be asking the questions that are found in this guide. Plan to share what God has taught you in your individual study.

3. Stick to the passage being studied. Your answers should be based on the verses which are the focus of the discussion and not on outside authorities such as commentaries or speakers. This guide deliberately avoids jumping

from book to book or passage to passage. Each study focuses on only one passage. Book studies are generally designed to lead you through the book in the order in which it was written. This will help you follow the author's argument.

4. Be sensitive to the other members of the group. Listen attentively when they share what they have learned. You may be surprised by their insights! Link what you say to the comments of others so the group stays on the topic. Also, be affirming whenever you can. This will encourage some of the more hesitant members of the group to participate.

5. Be careful not to dominate the discussion. We are sometimes so eager to share what we have learned that we leave too little opportunity for others to respond. By all means participate! But allow others to also.

6. Expect God to teach you through the passage being discussed and through the other members of the group. Pray that you will have an enjoyable and profitable time together.

7. If you are the discussion leader, you will find additional suggestions and helpful ideas for each study in the leader's notes. These are found at the back of the guide.

Introducing the Gospel of John

The most significant fact in history can be summed up in four words: *Jesus Christ is God!* The great declaration of the Bible is that God in human flesh was born in Bethlehem. It was God in the person of Jesus Christ who astonished the people of his day with his miracles and amazed them with his teaching. It was God who lived a perfect life and then allowed himself to be put to death on a Roman cross for humanity's sins. It was God who three days after he died broke the bonds of death and came out of the grave alive. The deity of Jesus—the fact that he was God in human flesh—is the bottom line of the Christian faith.

When the apostle John sat down to write his Gospel, he was not interested simply in adding one more biography of Jesus to the three already in existence. John wrote his book with a very specific purpose in mind. He tells us in 20:30-31:

> Jesus did many other miraculous signs in the presence of his disciples, which are not recorded in this book. But these are written that you may believe that Jesus is the Christ, the Son of God, and that by believing you may have life in his name.

John's book is not a biography; it's a theological argument. John wants to convince us that Jesus of Nazareth is God the Son. Then he wants to show us how that fact will change our lives in some rather amazing ways. It is by believing in Jesus Christ as the Son of God that we find life—real life, eternal life, a whole new kind of life!

Every event John records is designed to show us that Jesus is God. John pulls from the life of Jesus specific incidents that demonstrate his majesty and deity. Of particular interest to John are the sign miracles of Jesus. In the first twelve chapters of his book, John records seven miracles. These miracles were not performed simply to alleviate human suffering or to meet human need. The miracles were "signs." They pointed to the truth of Jesus' claim to be the Son of God.

John was the last Gospel writer. The best evidence points to a date around A.D. 90 for the composition of his Gospel. The other Gospels had been in circulation for some time. John wrote to add his unique perspective and to fill in some of the details not recorded by the other writers. He assumes his readers are familiar with the other Gospels. John does not mention, for example, the anguish of Jesus in the Garden of Gethsemane. The other writers had adequately described that incident. John does give us the details of Jesus' conversation with his disciples in the upper room. The other writers mention it only briefly.

John never mentions himself by name in the Gospel. He refers to himself simply as "the disciple whom Jesus loved." We have in this Gospel the memories of an intimate friend about the Lord Jesus. Jesus Christ had transformed John's life. I hope you are prepared to have that happen to you! You are about to begin a fascinating study focused on the greatest person who ever lived—Jesus Christ. If you will respond to what John writes in faith and obedience, you, like John, will experience a whole new kind of life.

Part 1
Jesus, the Living Word of God

John 1–12

1
The Master & Five Who Followed

John 1:1-51

It was a great day in our history when a man first walked on the moon. But the Bible declares that a far greater event took place two thousand years ago. God walked on the earth in the person of Jesus Christ. John opens his Gospel with a beautiful hymn of exaltation to Christ. It is one of the most profound passages in all the Bible. It is written in simple, straightforward language, yet in studying the depths of its meaning, it is a passage where we never reach bottom. It is an ocean-sized truth, and we have to be content to paddle around in shallow water.

1. What do you hope will happen in your life as a result of studying the Gospel of John?

2. Read John 1:1-18. Why do you think John calls Jesus *the Word* (see vv. 1, 14)?

3. In verses 1-3 what facts does John declare to be true of the Word?

Why are these facts significant for understanding who Jesus is?

4. What do the symbols of life (v. 4) and light (v. 5) tell us about Jesus and why he came to earth?

How has Jesus brought these qualities into your life?

5. John contrasts Jesus' rejection by the majority with his reception by a few (vv. 9-13). What facts about Jesus should have brought the majority to receive him (vv. 9-11)?

6. How would you explain to someone both the meaning and results of receiving Jesus (vv. 12-13)?

7. According to verses 14-18, what specific aspects of God's character are revealed to us through Jesus?

8. Read John 1:19-34. According to these verses, what steps did John take to guarantee that people would not look at him but at Christ?

9. How would you summarize John's testimony concerning Jesus?

10. Read John 1:35-51. In these verses we are introduced to five men: Andrew, Simon, Philip, Nathanael and one unnamed disciple (John). How did each man respond to the testimony he heard about Jesus?

Which of these responses have you encountered as you have shared your faith in Jesus Christ?

11. John records more than a dozen names or descriptions of Jesus in this chapter. What are some of these?

12. Which of the names of Jesus has the most significance to you personally? Explain why.

2
Wine &
a Whip
John 2:1-25

After I had given a presentation on the claims of Christ, a skeptical student asked: "What proof do you have that Jesus really was who he claimed to be?" People have been asking that question for two thousand years! For John the convincing proof of Jesus' deity was found in his words and deeds. No one but God could say the things Jesus said, and no one but God could do the things Jesus did.

In chapter two, John pulls two events from the early ministry of Jesus that demonstrate his power and authority. We are shown a miraculous sign as Jesus exercises his creative power to turn water into wine. We are also shown a prophetic sign as Jesus cleanses God's temple in Jerusalem. Both signs demonstrate that Jesus was the fullness of God clothed in humanity.

1. What initially convinced you that Jesus was more than a man?

2. Read John 2:1-11. When the groom's parents ran out of wine for their guests, Jesus' mother asked him to help (v. 3). What do you think Mary expected Jesus to do? (Remember, according to verse 11 Jesus had not yet performed any miracles.)

3. What did Jesus mean by his reply to Mary in verse 4?

4. In your opinion, why did Jesus command that the servants fill the pots with water (v. 7)? (Obviously, Jesus could have simply created wine in the empty pots.)

5. If you had been a wedding guest, what do you imagine your reaction would have been to this miracle?

How did Jesus' disciples respond (v. 11)?

6. According to verse 11, the purpose of Jesus' miracle was not to save the groom from embarrassment but to display Christ's glory. What aspects of Christ's glory does this miracle reveal to you?

7. Read John 2:12-25. How does John's picture of Jesus in verses 15-16 fit with today's popular concept of him?

8. What is the significance of Jesus' claim that the temple is "my Father's house" (v. 16)?

9. Only the Messiah had the authority to cleanse the temple. The people recognized that and asked Jesus for a miraculous sign to confirm his identity (v. 18). To what "sign" did Jesus point them (vv. 19-22)?

Why do you think that particular sign was so significant in Jesus' mind?

10. Why didn't the disciples immediately grasp what Jesus was talking about when he said, "Destroy this temple, and I will raise it again in three days" (vv. 19, 22)?

11. If people were believing in Jesus because of the miraculous signs, why didn't Jesus "entrust himself to them" (vv. 23-25)?

12. What do we learn from this passage about Jesus' concern for his Father's reputation?

13. In what practical ways can you demonstrate the same concern toward the holy character of God?

3
The New Birth

John 3:1-36

I talked today to a junior in college who is only one month old. No, she isn't a child genius. Recently a friend explained to her the claims of Christ. As she responded in simple faith, she experienced the joys of spiritual birth.

The most beautiful explanation of the new birth is found here in John 3. It's a passage that children can understand and one that the greatest saints of God have never fully grasped. It's a message not so much to be analyzed and dissected as it is to be received with joy.

1. What are some of the positive images associated with birth?

2. Read John 3:1-21. What is your impression of Nicodemus?

3. Why do you think he comes to see Jesus at night?

Why does he come to see Jesus at all?

---

4. Jesus' reply to Nicodemus (v. 3) seems to have nothing to do with Nicodemus's statement (v. 2). Why do you think Jesus brings up the subject of the new birth?

---

5. Why do you suppose Nicodemus responds to Jesus' explanation with such amazement (v. 9)?

---

6. Why is Jesus likewise amazed at Nicodemus's ignorance (vv. 10-12)?

---

7. How does the story of Moses lifting up the snake in the desert (vv. 14-15; see Num 21:4-9) illustrate our need and Christ's offer?

---

8. What impresses you about God's supreme act of love (vv. 16-17)?

---

9. How and why does our response to God's Son determine our destiny (vv. 18-21)?

10. This passage emphasizes the importance of our personal response to Jesus Christ. How would you describe your response?

11. Read John 3:22-36. In your opinion, what motivated John's disciples to raise the issue of Jesus' ministry?

12. How would you summarize John's view of the character and ministry of Jesus?

13. How did John demonstrate by his attitude and actions that Jesus was superior to him?

14. What is one way you can demonstrate Christ's superiority in your life?

4
Soul & Body— Saving & Healing
John 4:1-54

I love humanity; it's *people* I can't stand!" Those well-known words from a member of the "Peanuts" gang still make us chuckle. But our smiles hide the fact that we sometimes feel exactly like that. John says very little about Jesus' contact with the multitudes. But long sections of the Gospel are devoted to conversations Jesus had with individuals. Jesus was open, warm and vitally interested in people.

In John 4 we see Jesus reach out first to a woman, then to his disciples, and finally to a grieving father. Watching Jesus give himself to people with love and compassion will help us care for those God puts in our paths.

1. When have you been able to turn an ordinary conversation into a discussion about Christ?

2. Read John 4:1-26. Why do you think Jesus "had to go through Samaria" on his way to Galilee (v. 4)? (Jews normally went around Samaria to avoid contact with the hated Samaritans.)

3. What is surprising about Jesus' question to the Samaritan woman (vv. 8-9)?

What present-day situations might arouse the same racial, religious and sexual prejudices?

4. How does Jesus' offer of "living water" contrast with what the woman thinks he means (vv. 10-15)?

What does this offer of "living water" mean in your life and experience?

5. Why do you think Jesus brings up the woman's long list of past marriages and her present adulterous relationship (vv. 16-18)?

6. Why does the woman suddenly change the subject and begin talking about the controversy over the proper place of worship (vv. 19-20)?

7. How does Jesus handle her question about this Samaritan-Jewish controversy (vv. 21-24)?

8. What principles can you draw from Jesus' conversation with the woman to help you in discussing the gospel with non-Christians?

9. Read John 4:27-42. From your reading of this passage, do you think the Samaritan woman genuinely believed? What do you see in the passage that supports your position?

10. How is the disciples' confusion about food (vv. 31-33) similar to the woman's confusion about living water?

11. After his encounter with the Samaritan woman, what specific lessons does Jesus apply to his disciples and to us (vv. 34-38)?

12. Read John 4:43-54. How does the royal official's attitude toward Jesus differ from the response Jesus had already anticipated (see v. 44)?

---

13. What does this "second miraculous sign" Jesus performed (v. 54) reveal about him?

---

14. What has Jesus taught you in this chapter about meeting the specific needs of those around you?

5
Deity on Trial
John 5:1-47

In my high-school years, I was hooked on television lawyer programs. Those intrepid men and women always found the missing piece of evidence that would rescue the innocent and convict the guilty. I've learned since high-school days that sometimes judges and juries are wrong. Men and women may hear all the testimony and still make a wrong decision.

In John chapter five Jesus is on trial. It is not a formal trial in a courtroom, but all the elements of a trial appear in the story. A group of people are forced to make a decision about Jesus in their hearts. They hear all the evidence but make a disastrously wrong decision. Judgments are still made for and against Jesus. Whenever he is presented as Savior and Lord, people decide in their hearts to believe his claims or to turn and walk away.

1. What are some reasons why people reject Jesus Christ?

2. Read John 5:1-15. Based on the scene and conversation around the pool, how would you describe the feelings and attitudes of the invalid?

3. How do you think the man felt after his healing?

4. The seventh commandment said: "Remember the Sabbath day by keeping it holy" (see Ex 20:8-11). In their zeal to apply this command, what were the Jews failing to see (Jn 5:9-15)?

5. When have you been more concerned about a religious activity than the reality behind it? Explain.

6. Read John 5:16-30. Jesus explains that the work of creation ended on the seventh day, but not the work of compassion (vv. 16-18). Why does his explanation make the Jews even more determined to kill him?

7. What insights do verses 19-23 give us into (a) the Father's devotion to the Son and (b) the Son's dependence on the Father?

8. According to Jesus, why is our response to him a matter of eternal life or death (vv. 24-30)?

9. Read John 5:31-47. What "witnesses" does Jesus call forward to testify on his behalf?

How does their testimony validate his claims?

10. What counter-accusations does Jesus make against those who are attacking him?

Why would each one be a severe blow to the religious piety of these Jewish listeners?

11. How can we avoid the kind of religion that is outwardly pious but inwardly bankrupt?

12. According to this chapter, what really influences our verdict for or against Jesus?

6
Jesus,
the Bread of Life
John 6:1-71

Do you realize that during your lifetime you will probably spend over thirty-five thousand hours eating? That's the equivalent of eight years of non-stop meals, twelve hours a day! The problem, of course, is that even after a big meal we get hungry again. At best, food only satisfies us for a few hours.

Yet in this chapter, Jesus offers us food that satisfies our hunger forever. You can't buy it in a grocery store. It is found only in Jesus himself.

1. How do you usually respond to an "impossible" situation—a problem in your life that doesn't seem to have a solution?

2. Read John 6:1-15. How would you characterize Philip's and Andrew's response to the problem of feeding this enormous crowd (vv. 5-9)?

3. If Jesus knew what he was going to do (v. 6), why do you think he asked these two disciples for advice?

4. How do you think the disciples felt as they gathered up the pieces left over (vv. 12-13)?

5. What insights does this passage give you into how Christ may be at work in the difficult situations in your life?

6. Read John 6:16-42. Imagine that you are one of the disciples, rowing the boat in dark, rough waters (vv. 16-21). How would your concept of Jesus have been altered by seeing him walk on water?

7. The next day the people were hungry again, so they came seeking Jesus (vv. 22-25). How does he try to redirect their thinking (vv. 26-33)?

8. How does Jesus' claim to be the bread of life (v. 35) relate to his miraculous feeding of the five thousand (vv. 1-13)?

9. Based on the remarks of some in the crowd (vv. 41-42), do you think they finally understood what Jesus was saying? Explain.

10. Read John 6:43-59. When Jesus said, "This bread is my flesh," the crowd could think only of cannibalism (v. 52). What do you think it means to eat

Jesus' flesh and drink his blood (vv. 53-59)?

Is this something we do once for all time, or is it an ongoing process? Explain.

11. Read John 6:60-71. In these verses Jesus turns away from the crowd and focuses on his disciples. How would you describe their responses to his "hard teaching"?

Which response best describes your present attitude toward Jesus? Explain.

12. Jesus has contrasted the two appetites found in every person—the appetite for food that perishes and the appetite for food that endures. In what ways has Jesus satisfied the spiritual hunger in your heart?

7
Confusion over Christ

John 7:1-52

N ot long ago I had a series of conversations with a young man about Jesus Christ and why faith in him is so important. At first, the young man was interested. He was open to listen to God's Word and to consider Christ's claims. As time went on, however, he became more and more hostile to Christ. Finally, he told me that he didn't want to pursue his investigation any further. He had decided to reject Christ and his offer of salvation.

That is precisely the pattern that John traces in his Gospel. In the early chapters, men and women responded to Jesus with belief. Then some of those who were following him turned away. Now open warfare breaks out between Jesus and his enemies—and yet, some still seek the truth. This chapter will help you respond positively to the wide variety of attitudes toward Jesus today.

---

1. Have you ever had to work with someone who disliked or even hated you? What was it like to face that person every day? (Or what do you think it would be like?)

---

2. Read John 7:1-13. The first blast of hostility against Jesus comes from his own family. How would you characterize the statements made by Jesus' brothers?

3. Why do you think Jesus waits to go to Jerusalem until after his brothers have left (v. 10)?

4. What counsel would you give a believer who faces spiritual opposition from his or her family?

V 25

5. Read John 7:14-52. When Jesus makes his presence in Jerusalem known, people begin to challenge the origin (and, therefore, the authority) of his teaching. According to Jesus, how can we verify the truth of his teaching (vv. 16-18)?

6. What other opinions or questions do people have about Jesus in verses 20-36?

How does Jesus respond to each one?

7. On the last day of the Feast of Tabernacles, large vats of water were poured out on the pavement of the temple court as a reminder of God's provision of water in the wilderness. With that custom in mind, how would you explain the significance of Jesus' remarks in verses 37-39?

To what extent has Christ been a continual source of spiritual refreshment for you? Why or why not?

8. Throughout the chapter John gives us a sampling of various reactions to Jesus. Identify some of the reactions of various people and explain why you think they reacted the way they did.

9. Which of the opinions you have identified in this chapter are still expressed today, and in what way?

10. Based on Jesus' example, what should our response be to such reactions?

8
Caught in Adultery
John 7:53—8:11

Nothing is more humiliating than being caught in an act of disobedience! Whether it's a child with his hand in the cookie jar or an adult driving over the speed limit, we all know the sinking feeling of being caught. In John 8, a woman is caught in the most awkward of situations—in the very act of adultery. The way Jesus responds to her may surprise you.

1. Think of a time when you hurt someone and that person was willing to forgive you. How did it feel to be forgiven?

2. Read John 7:53—8:11. What do we know about the character and motives of those who bring this woman to Jesus?

3. How do you think the woman feels when the men make her "stand before the group" and publicly expose her sin?

4. How do you feel when someone exposes a sin in your life—either privately or publicly?

5. While it is obvious that the woman is guilty, what elements of injustice can you find in this situation?

6. In your opinion, what was Jesus writing in the dirt?

7. The Pharisees and teachers were often very self-righteous. Why do you think they went away rather than stoning the woman (vv. 7-9)?

8. Why are we tempted to condemn other people's sins rather than our own?

9. How would you describe Jesus' attitude toward the woman (vv. 10-11)?

10. Do you think Jesus was condoning the woman's sin by not condemning her? Explain.

11. If you were the woman, how would you feel as you left Jesus' presence?

12. What can we learn from this passage about Christ's attitude toward us—even when we feel awful about ourselves?

What does it teach us about forgiving and accepting others?

9
Jesus, the Light of the World

John 8:12-59

Jesus never spoke in public without creating controversy. In fact, he was constantly in trouble! Rather than retreating behind the safety of a pulpit, Jesus spoke in settings where people were bold enough to talk back. In this portion of John's story, Jesus makes a series of claims about himself. Each claim is met by a challenge from his enemies. Each challenge is then answered and the answer leads to the next claim. Throughout this interchange, Jesus shows us how to speak the truth in the face of hostility. He also reveals some amazing things about himself.

1. Have you ever tried to talk about Christ with a family member or co-worker who was hostile to your message? How did you feel at the time?

How did you try to penetrate that person's spiritual barriers?

2. Read John 8:12-30. Jesus' first claim is: "I am the light of the world. Whoever follows me will never walk in darkness, but will have the light of life." What does it mean to walk in darkness (v. 12)?

How has following Jesus brought light into your life?

3. The Pharisees challenge the validity of Jesus' claim (v. 13; see Deut 19:15). How does Jesus answer their challenge (vv. 14-18)?

4. Jesus' reference to his Father leads to his second claim—that he came from God. How does this claim heighten the tension between Jesus and the Jews (vv. 19-30)?

5. It seems as if Jesus is deliberately provoking the Jews by what he says. Why do you think he is being so blunt?

6. Read John 8:31-59. Jesus makes another startling claim in verses 31-32: "If you hold to my teaching. . . then you will know the truth, and the truth will set you free." Why does holding to Jesus' teaching lead to true knowledge and freedom?

7. Those who had believed interrupted to say that they were already free.

What analysis does Jesus give of their "freedom" (vv. 34-36)?

8. Jesus' opponents also claim to have both Abraham and God as their father. According to Jesus, how does their conduct contradict their claim (vv. 39-47)?

9. Why is our conduct the truest test of our beliefs?

10. What is it about Jesus' statements that make his enemies want to stone him (vv. 48-59)?

11. Summarize the various attacks voiced against Jesus in this chapter and explain how Jesus' example will help you face spiritually hostile people.

12. In what ways does your lifestyle validate (or invalidate) your claim to be a follower of Christ?

10
A Blind Man Sees the Light

John 9:1-41

Our sight is a wonderful gift from God. We marvel at the fiery colors of a sunset, the rich pastels of spring and the delicate beauty of a flower. How tragic it must be to never see the light of day.

Yet there is a far greater tragedy than physical blindness. In this passage Jesus meets a man who has been blind from birth. The man illustrates that those who are blind often see clearly, while those with sight see nothing at all.

1. If you could have any of the powers that Jesus had to do good, which would you choose and why?

2. Read John 9:1-12. Based on the question the disciples ask Jesus (v. 2), how do they view the relation between sickness and sin?

What is Jesus' view of the same issue?

3. In your opinion, which of these views is more widely held among Christians today? Explain.

4. In verse 5 Jesus claims to be the light of the world. In what sense does the physical healing of the blind man confirm his spiritual claim?

5. Why do you think Jesus goes through the process of making mud and instructing the man to go wash, instead of simply healing him instantly?

6. Read John 9:13-41. On what grounds do the Pharisees object to this miracle (vv. 16, 22, 24, 29)?

7. Still skeptical, the Jews send for the man's parents (v. 18). How would you describe the parents' attitude and response (vv. 19-23)?

8. How do the Pharisees react when the genuineness of the miracle becomes undeniable (vv. 28-34)?

9. When might Christians today exhibit the Pharisees' attitude to a marvelous work of God's grace or power?

10. How would you describe the various emotions this man must have had as he moved from being healed by Jesus through the questioning and final rejection by the Pharisees?

11. What is Jesus' purpose in seeking out the healed man the second time (vv. 35-38)?

12. Throughout this chapter, how have the Pharisees exhibited the kind of stubborn spiritual blindness Jesus describes in verses 39-41?

13. What principles in this chapter could help us improve our spiritual eyesight?

11
The Shepherd & His Sheep
John 10:1-42

J esus was a master at using simple, everyday objects or events to illustrate profound spiritual truths. The farmer scattering seed, the vine sustaining the branches, and sparrows falling to the earth all took on a new dimension in Jesus' eyes. In John 10, Jesus uses the scene of a shepherd enclosing his sheep in a sheepfold to give us one of the most moving pictures of our salvation and security in Christ found anywhere in the Bible. If you've ever doubted the love of Christ, Jesus will give you a healthy dose of assurance in this chapter.

---

1. What usually prompts you to have doubts about your salvation or your walk with Christ--your own sin? feelings of unworthiness? personal failures? Explain.

---

2. Read John 10:1-21. Jesus uses the picture of the sheepfold as a "figure of speech" (v. 6). What spiritual truths is Jesus trying to convey (vv. 1-5)?

3. What does Jesus mean when he describes himself as "the gate for the sheep" (vv. 7-10)?

4. In verses 11-15 Jesus talks about the shepherd's care for his sheep. What can you learn from those verses about Jesus' care and relationship with you?

5. What does Jesus reveal about the future of his flock (v. 16)?

In what ways do you feel a part of "one flock" under "one shepherd"?

6. Why do you think Jesus stresses that he lays down his life of his own accord (vv. 17-18)?

7. Read John 10:22-42. According to Jesus, how are the Jews in this passage different from his sheep (vv. 22-27)?

8. Jesus calls his followers *sheep.* What impressions (positive and negative) does the picture of sheep bring to your mind?

9. How do you respond to promises and assurances Jesus gives his sheep in verses 28-29?

10. When Jesus claims that he and the Father are one, the Jews pick up stones to stone him (vv. 30-33). Do you think his defense is a denial of his deity (vv. 33-36)? Explain.

11. Which promise from Jesus in this chapter is most encouraging to you?

How can that promise help you with your answer to question 1?

12
Resurrection & Life
John 11:1-57

Ever since God judged Adam and Eve, death has plagued humanity. It separates us from those we love and looms over our own lives like a menacing spirit. In this chapter Jesus reaches out to a family struggling with the pain of death. He shows us why we need never fear death again.

1. Think back to the death of a family member or friend. Did that death cause you to question God's love? Explain.

2. Read John 11:1-44. How can we resolve the seeming conflict between Jesus' love for Lazarus and his deliberate delay in helping him (vv. 4-5)?

3. How can those verses help us when we feel abandoned by God in a time of great need?

4. What additional insight into God's purposes can we gain from Jesus' statement in verse 15?

5. What elements of doubt and faith do you see in Martha's statements to Jesus (vv. 17-27)?

How does Jesus stretch Martha's faith in this brief encounter?

6. Jesus declares to Martha that "he who believes in me will live, even though he dies; and whoever lives and believes in me will never die" (vv. 25-26). What kind of "life" and "death" is Jesus referring to in each case?

How should Christ's statement radically alter our views of life and death?

7. Why do you think John emphasizes that Jesus was deeply moved by Mary's grief and the anguish of those with her (vv. 28-38)?

8. Based on this passage, how would you respond to those who believe that grief is incompatible with real faith?

9. Read John 11:45-57. How would you explain the fact that the people who see the same miracle respond in two totally different ways?

10. What does this account reveal about the value of miracles for bringing people to faith in Christ?

11. In what ways will this chapter change the way you respond to personal difficulty or the apparent delay of God?

13
The King's Last Acts

John 12:1-50

Ⅰf you have ever felt rejected or misunderstood, you know how Jesus felt as his public ministry came to an end. The hostility against him had risen to a fever pitch. His gentle compassion and abundant miracles were met with oppression and violence. Jesus knew what none of his friends knew—that he was about to die. In spite of the fleeting attempts of the crowd to make him King, Jesus chose the way of the cross.

1. If you knew for sure that you had only one week to live, what would you do with that week?

2. Read John 12:1-11. What motivates Mary to pour expensive perfume on Jesus' feet?

3. Judas objects to Mary's extravagance. What motives and wrong thinking lie behind his objection (vv. 4-8)?

4. In what ways should we be extravagant in our devotion to Jesus?

5. Read John 12:12-36. What do the shouts of the crowd tell us about their expectations of Jesus (vv. 12-19)?

6. How do Christ's statements about his mission clash with the crowd's expectations (vv. 23-28)?

7. Jesus often used apparent contradictions to drive home a truth. How would you explain verse 25 in terms that apply to your life (see also vv. 26-28)?

8. Jesus makes it clear that he is about to die. According to verses 23-33, what will Jesus' death accomplish (note vv. 23-24, 28, 31-32)?

Which of these results is most encouraging to you? Explain.

9. Read John 12:37-50. When we stubbornly refuse to believe, what happens to our spiritual senses, and why (vv. 37-41)?

10. Although some of the leaders "believe" in Jesus (vv. 42-43), how are they like the man who loves his life and loses it (see v. 25)?

11. Jesus' last public message to his people is recorded in verses 44-50. What indications do you find that he is still reaching out in love and grace to those who have rejected him?

How can you apply the example of Jesus to people who reject you or your testimony about Christ?

12. In your own life are you more interested in earthly acclaim and glory or are you willing to lose your life for Christ's sake? Examine your direction and life goals in the light of Jesus' commitment to do the will of the Father.

Part 2
Jesus, the Living Way to God

John 13—21

1
The Son as a Slave

John 13:1-17

T here were two things on Jesus' heart the night before his crucifixion—his Father and his disciples. In John 13—17, we have the privilege of listening to his conversations with them both. However, before Jesus can instruct his disciples about his death, he has to act out a lesson in servitude. Jesus also shows us the spirit he expects in those who follow him. Greatness in Christ's eyes does not come from having many servants but from being the servant of many.

1. Have you ever been asked to do a demeaning, lowly job? What thoughts went through your mind at that time?

2. Read John 13:1-17. According to John, what did Jesus know about himself (vv. 1-3)?

In light of that knowledge, what is remarkable about what Jesus did next (vv. 4-5)?

4. Footwashing was normally done by servants or slaves. Why do you think Jesus washed his disciples' feet instead of simply talking to them about love?

---

5. What tasks at home, at work or in church would be equivalent to foot-washing?

---

6. How do you think Jesus felt as he washed Judas's feet?

How do you think Judas felt?

---

7. Was Peter simply being humble when he refused to allow Jesus to serve him (vv. 6-8)? Explain.

---

8. What spiritual truth was Jesus trying to communicate to Peter (and to us) in verses 8-11?

---

9. Like Peter, do you ever feel awkward or uncomfortable when others try to serve you? Explain.

10. After he had finished washing the disciples' feet, how did Jesus explain the significance of his actions (vv. 12-17)?

11. Based on Jesus' words in verse 17, how would you describe the relationship between knowledge, action and joy in the Christian life?

12. What has this chapter revealed to you about your attitude toward serving?

13. In what specific ways can you model the humility of Jesus toward those with whom you live or work?

2
The Betrayer
& the Boaster
John 13:18-38

T here are some people we just don't like to be around! They aren't necessarily our enemies. They simply have the uncanny ability to irritate us. If we had been one of Jesus' disciples, we would probably have found it difficult to be around Peter. He was blunt and, at times, arrogant. On the other hand, we might have regarded Judas with trust and respect. The only one who saw deeply enough to discern the true character of these men was Jesus.

1. Has someone in your life ever hurt you deeply? What was your response to him or her?

2. Read John 13:18-30. Jesus takes this opportunity to predict his betrayal. How would his prediction dispel any doubts the disciples might have and strengthen their faith (v. 19)?

3. Evidently, the disciples did not know who would betray Jesus (v. 22). What does this tell us about how Jesus had treated Judas?

4. How would you have treated Judas if you knew he would eventually betray you?

5. How do the disciples interpret Jesus' instruction to Judas in verse 27 (vv. 28-29)?

6. Can we apply Jesus' example to the way we should treat our "betrayers," or was this a unique situation that really doesn't apply today? Explain.

7. Read John 13:31-38. What was "new" about Jesus' command in verse 34?

8. John later wrote: "This is how we know what love is: Jesus Christ laid down his life for us. And we ought to lay down our lives for our brothers" (1 Jn 3:16). In what practical ways can we exhibit this sacrificial love?

9. Why does that kind of love convince all of humanity that we are Jesus' disciples (v. 35)?

10. Do you think Peter's declaration in verse 37 comes from pride or from sincerity? Explain.

11. Three people stand out in this passage—Jesus, Judas and Peter. What one character quality of each—good or evil—impresses you the most?

What can you do to avoid the failures and to follow after the strengths of each of them?

3
Comfort for a Troubled Heart

John 14:1-31

T he call came late at night. A broken sob was followed by these words: "Our son is dying. Will you please come to the hospital?" As I made the trip through darkened streets, I wondered what I could say to bring comfort to these heartbroken parents. Jesus faced that challenge too. In this chapter he comforts eleven disciples who feel like their world is coming unglued.

---

1. Think of a friend who is going through a personal crisis. If you were with that person now, how would you try to help him or her?

---

2. Read John 14:1-13. What had Jesus said in chapter 13 to cause his disciples to have "troubled" hearts (v. 1)?

---

3. In your opinion, how would the promises Jesus makes in verses 1-4 bring comfort to his disciples?

4. After being with Jesus for over three years, what have both Thomas and Phillip failed to realize about him (vv. 5-14)?

5. In light of verses 5-14, why is it crucial for our focus to be on Jesus himself?

6. Read John 14:15-31. Another source of comfort for these troubled disciples would be the Holy Spirit. What does the title *Counselor* tell us about the Spirit's ministry?

7. According to Jesus, how will the Spirit bring comfort and help to his followers (vv. 15-27)?

8. In what specific ways has the Spirit brought comfort or help in your life?

9. What is the relationship between our love and obedience to Jesus and his love and presence in our lives (vv. 15-24)?

How is this different from legalism—earning Christ's love and presence through our good works?

_____

10. How does the peace Christ offers differ from that which the world offers (vv. 25-31)?

_____

11. We began this study by thinking about friends who are going through times of trouble or pain. What help has this chapter given you for ministering to them?

_____

12. How can Jesus' words help you in a personal crisis or when you have a troubled heart?

4
The Secret of Remaining
John 15:1-11

The final weekend before Christmas is not the time to visit a shopping mall. If you are fortunate enough to find a parking spot, the press of people inside makes shopping almost impossible. One mother was giving final instructions to her young son before plunging into the crowd: "Stay close to me and hold my hand all the time. We won't get separated if we hold on to each other."

As Jesus prepared his disciples to face life without his visible presence, he impressed on them the importance of staying close to him spiritually. He said, "Remain in me." If you've ever longed to understand the secret of spiritual growth, you will find it in Jesus' words to us in John 15.

---

1. Have you ever felt far from Christ since becoming a Christian? What circumstances made you feel that way?

---

2. Read John 15:1-11. Jesus' instruction to his disciples in this passage revolve around three symbols—the vine, the gardener and the branches. What is Jesus trying to communicate by calling himself the *true vine?*

3. What is the significance of calling his disciples *branches?*

4. Instead of commanding us to bear fruit, why is Jesus' only command "Remain in me" (v. 4)?

5. What does it mean to remain in Christ?

6. The fruit produced by the remaining branch is often viewed as a reference to new converts. But branches produce grapes, not other branches. What other possible meanings are there for *fruit?*

7. The Father's ministry as the gardener is to "cut off every branch . . . that bears no fruit" (v. 2). What do you think that means?

8. The Father prunes fruitful branches to make them more fruitful (v. 2). In what ways have you experienced the Father's "pruning"?

What were the results?

10. What spiritual benefits result from remaining in Christ (vv. 7-11)?

11. There are three categories of branches described in this passage—those bearing no fruit, those bearing some fruit, and those bearing much fruit. In which category would you place yourself and why?

12. If you are not bearing much fruit, what is Jesus' counsel to you in these verses?

5
The Cost of Friendship
John 15:12–16:4

While on earth, Jesus did not surround himself with a group of students or even a group of followers. He placed himself in the company of friends. To admit that we need friends is a sign of maturity, not immaturity. Close relationships are Christlike! In this passage Jesus shows us what friendship with him is really like. There's both comfort and cost.

1. In your opinion, what are some of the most important qualities in a friendship?

2. Read John 15:12-17. Jesus' command in verse 12 is, "Love each other as I have loved you." In what specific ways did Jesus demonstrate his love?

In what practical ways can we, like Christ, lay down our lives for our friends?

3. What are the requirements and benefits of friendship with Christ (vv. 14-17)?

4. Is being a friend of Jesus the same as being a believer in Jesus? Explain.

5. Read John 15:18-25. If love is to characterize our relationship with other believers, hate will characterize our relationship with the world. What reasons does Jesus give for the world's hatred?

6. Give one or two specific examples of how you have experienced the world's hatred as a Christian.

How did you respond to the hostility at the time?

7. What does Jesus mean when he says that without his coming, his words and his miracles, the world "would not be guilty of sin" (vv. 22-25)?

8. Read John 15:26—16:4. In what specific ways will the Counselor and the disciples themselves continue the ministry begun by Jesus (vv. 26-27)?

9. What kind of treatment can the disciples expect from those who do not know Christ (16:1-4)?

10. What kinds of persecution are most probable for us in our society? Explain.

11. If we as Christians are not persecuted in some way, what might that imply about our spiritual commitment?

6
Secrets
of the Spirit
John 16:5-15

Alovely woman in our church died not long ago. She knew for almost a year that, unless the Lord intervened, the cancer in her brain would kill her. That year gave her time of wonderful interaction with her husband and family. Her family had the opportunity to express their love for her, and the dying woman had the privilege of passing on her godly wisdom.

In John 16 Jesus knows that he will die in less than twenty-four hours. When his disciples are faced with that reality, they become troubled (14:1), afraid (14:27) and filled with grief (16:6). Jesus responds to each of their concerns by talking about the coming Holy Spirit.

1. What would you want to tell your family or closest friends if you knew that you had only a short time to live?

2. Read John 16:5-15. Jesus said that it was for the disciples' good that he go away and that the Counselor come. Why was the Spirit's presence more profitable to the disciples than Jesus' presence?

3. In what ways is it more profitable today to have the Holy Spirit actively present than to have Jesus here on earth? Explain.

4. What did Jesus say the Spirit's ministry would be toward the world (vv. 8-11)?

5. How does the Spirit do the same work in the hearts of unbelievers today?

6. "The prince of this world" mentioned in verse 11 is Satan. In what way does Satan "now stand condemned"?

7. Why is it important for the Holy Spirit to convince the world that their "prince" is already condemned?

8. What can we infer from verses 8-11 about our part in evangelism?

9. The Spirit's ministry is one of communication. What specific things did Jesus say the Spirit would communicate to the disciples?

10. In what ways does the Spirit guide us into all truth and bring glory to Jesus Christ today?

7
A Dying Leader's Last Command

John 16:16-33

Those who believe in Christ are not shielded from life's deepest problems. We must still face sorrow, rejection and heartache. We see our loved ones die. We sometimes feel alone and unloved. We see our marriages fail or our children go their own way rather than God's way. Jesus gives us some very practical help in these verses for facing life's crises. He doesn't answer all our questions, but he gives us what we need to survive.

1. How do you tend to react in the midst of a personal crisis?

2. Read John 16:16-24. It is obvious that the disciples are confused and concerned about Jesus' statements (vv. 16-18). Why do you think they are confused?

3. Jesus answers their questions, not by giving them an explanation but by making them a promise (vv. 19-22). What was the promise?

Why would it bring them joy in the midst of their grief and confusion?

4. How can this incident help us when our questions to the Lord seemingly go unanswered?

5. What new promise regarding prayer does Jesus give his disciples (vv. 23-24)?

How would this promise make their joy complete?

6. What connection can you make for your own life between problems, prayer and joy?

7. Read John 16:25-33. How would Jesus' assurance of the Father's love help the disciples in the days just ahead of them?

8. In verse 32 Jesus predicts that his disciples will abandon him. How do you think that failure affected their feelings of self-worth?

How does failure affect you?

9. How would Jesus' promise of peace and victory (v. 33) sustain them through that failure?

10. Which of the promises in this chapter have made the deepest impression on you? Why?

11. How can these promises strengthen your heart during the trials and discouragements of the future?

8
The Master's Final Prayer
John 17:1-26

Trim he approach of death has a way of bringing our priorities into focus. People who know death is imminent also know what is really important in life and who they really care about. In Jesus' final prayer with his disciples, he prays for himself, for them and for you! Every believer is on Jesus' mind as he faces the greatest trial of his life—the cross.

1. What specific people would you want around you in a crisis, and why?

2. Read John 17:1-5. Jesus makes only one request for himself—that the Father would glorify him, so that he might glorify the Father. In what way would each one glorify the other?

Why do you think that was so important to Jesus?

3. To what extent is God's glory foremost in your mind on a daily basis? Explain.

4. How is Jesus' definition of eternal life (v. 3) different from merely living forever?

In what ways do you actively seek to know the Father and the Son better?

5. Read John 17:6-19. According to these verses, what specific ministries did Jesus have toward his disciples?

6. Twice Jesus asked the Father to protect his disciples from the evil one (vv. 11, 15). Why would that protection have been so important in Jesus' mind as he faced the cross?

7. Jesus also asked the Father to sanctify his disciples through his word (v. 17). How can we allow God's Word to have that kind of effect on our lives?

8. Read John 17:20-26. Jesus prayed that those who believe in him would be one, "so that the world may believe that you have sent me" (vv. 21, 23)? Why is our unity a powerful argument for the reality of Jesus?

9. In what practical ways can we demonstrate our oneness with other believers?

10. Jesus obviously prayed this prayer out loud to bring comfort and assurance to his disciples. In what particular ways do Jesus' words encourage or assure you?

11. How do the concerns that were on Jesus' heart as he faced death match up with the concerns that would be on your heart if you were facing death?

How would you account for the difference?

9
"Jesus, You're under Arrest!"
John 18:1-27

Most of us would hate the thought of being arrested and brought to trial. If we were guilty of a crime, being arrested would be humiliating. But if we were innocent, it would be devastating. Yet in what should have been a demeaning experience for Jesus, we see again his majesty and glory. Jesus uses an experience of attack, betrayal and abandonment to demonstrate his confident trust in the Father. His calm assurance will help us face life's hurts and injustices with the same trust in the same Father.

1. How would you respond if a group of people falsely accused you of a crime and even called the police to have you arrested?

2. Read John 18:1-14. Why would Jesus go to a place where Judas knew he might be found (vv. 1-3)?

3. When the soldiers say they are seeking Jesus of Nazareth, Jesus replies "I am he" (lit. "I am"; v. 5). How would you explain the reaction of the soldiers (v. 6)?

4. If you had been one of Jesus' disciples, what feelings would you have had when the soldiers arrived at the garden?

5. Based on Peter's reaction (v. 10), what were his feelings?

6. What insight do Peter's action and Jesus' rebuke (v. 11) give you about our attempts at times to "help God out" in our own strength and wisdom?

7. Read John 18:15-27. Think back to the deepest sin of your life. How does a look at your own sin change your attitude toward Peter's denial of Jesus?

8. What contrasts do you see between Jesus' and Peter's response to this crisis?

What factors made the difference in each man's response?

9. When your faith or commitment to Christ is challenged, which of the two men are you most like? Explain.

10. What can we learn from Peter's failure about being ready to stand against the world's challenges?

11. What specific events in this passage display (a) Jesus' courage, (b) his power and (c) his obedience to the Father?

Which attitude of Jesus in this section impresses you most?

12. How will this study change the way you will face a time of testing in your own life?

10
Pilate
on Trial
John 18:28—19:16

Christ Killers!" The words made my stomach tighten. Someone had spray-painted the words and a series of swastikas on the Jewish synagogue in our city. Anti-Semitism had raised its ugly head again.

The New Testament does blame the Jewish leaders for condemning Jesus to die. But they weren't acting alone. The Roman governor, Pontius Pilate, also condemned Jesus to die. He did so even though he knew that Jesus was innocent. There is a sense, too, in which we killed Jesus. He died for our sins and in our place. The most amazing answer to the question of who killed Jesus is that no one did! Jesus said, "No one takes my life from me. I lay it down of my own choice."

---

1. To what extent are you tempted to compromise your Christian faith or witness because of peer pressure?

---

2. Read John 18:28-38. How do the Jewish leaders reveal their hypocrisy by refusing to enter Pilate's (a Gentile) home (v. 28)?

3. A Roman trial included four basic elements: the accusation, the interrogation (search for evidence), the defense and the verdict. What events or statements from the text are included in each?

(a) The accusation:

(b) The interrogation:

(c) The defense:

(d) The verdict:

4. How would you describe Jesus' "kingdom" based on his response to Pilate (v. 36)?

5. Read John 18:39—19:16. Pilate obviously was trying to release Jesus. What specific attempts did he make?

How does it make you feel when you read the record of injustice done toward Jesus?

---

6. What can you conclude about Pilate's character after reading this passage? What kind of man was he?

---

7. The Jews' true charge against Jesus comes out in verse 7—"He claimed to be the Son of God." Why do you think Pilate reacted to that statement as he did (vv. 8-9)?

---

8. Why didn't Jesus say more to Pilate (vv. 9-11)? Shouldn't he have defended himself more vigorously?

---

9. What parallels can you draw between the crowd's threats toward Pilate (v. 12) and the world's attempts to detour Christians from fully following Christ?

10. The message of the Gospel is that Jesus took upon himself the condemnation that we deserve. In what specific ways do you see Christ's grace demonstrated in his trial before Pilate?

How can you respond appropriately to Christ's grace to you?

11
Obedient to Death

John 19:17-42

There is nothing pleasant or attractive about an execution. The only one I've ever seen was in a televised news report from Vietnam. A captured soldier was shot. It left a knot in my stomach for days.

In Jesus' day execution was designed to be public and painful. The account of the crucifixion is not easy to read. You may be tempted to think that Jesus' death was a cruel mistake. It wasn't. Jesus' life was not taken from him; he laid it down willingly. It was part of his plan—a plan that included you and me. His cross was in a very real sense our cross.

1. When you think about death, what feelings and thoughts come to mind?

2. Read John 19:17-27. Crucifixion was obviously a brutal and tortuous form of execution. Why do you think John leaves so much of the agonizing detail out of his account?

3. Three groups were involved in Jesus' death—the soldiers, the Jewish leaders and Pilate. How would you characterize each one's attitude toward Jesus?

In what ways do their attitudes toward Jesus parallel those of men and women today?

4. How do you think Mary, Jesus' mother, felt as she stood by the cross?

5. How is Jesus' tender care for her evident even while he is dying (vv. 26-27)?

6. Read John 19:28-42. What was the significance of Jesus' cry, "It is finished" (v. 30; see Jn 17:4)?

7. What evidence does John give that Jesus really died?

8. Why was it so important for John to establish the certainty of Jesus' death?

9. What feelings and thoughts would have gone through your mind if you had helped prepare Jesus for burial?

10. Where were Jesus' disciples during his crucifixion and burial (see Jn 16:32)?

Why do you think they were so conspicuously absent?

11. Under the same circumstances, do you think you would have been more like Joseph and Nicodemus or Jesus' disciples? Explain.

12. When it comes to public identification with Jesus, how is it possible to respond in the same ways today?

13. What aspect of Jesus' death has made the deepest impression on you, and why?

12
The Son Is Up!

John 20:1-31

The story circulated for days in the hospital where my brother worked. An orderly was told to take a body to the morgue. Simply out of habit, the orderly felt the man's wrist for a pulse. When he realized his mistake, the orderly quickly dropped the arm, but not before his sensitive fingers told him something his mind struggled to believe. There was a pulse! The doctors were called, and the man revived.

That story may or may not be true. But I know of one account of a man coming back to life that is true. The man lived for years after the event. In fact, he is still alive, as we will see in this passage.

---

1. How would you react if a friend told you he had seen someone raised from the dead?

---

2. Read John 20:1-31. John records three witnesses to the empty tomb: Mary Magdalene, Peter and "the other disciple" (John himself). What important details do we learn from each one (vv. 1-9)?

3. Why is it important to prove the tomb was empty?

4. John also records three appearances of the risen Christ: to Mary, to his disciples and to Thomas. Why do you think Mary doesn't immediately recognize Jesus (vv. 10-15)?

After she does recognize him, what impresses you most about their encounter (vv. 16-18)?

5. When Jesus appears to his disciples, what specific gifts and promises does he give them (vv. 19-23)?

What do you think is the significance of each gift or promise?

6. Finally, Jesus appears to Thomas (vv. 24-29). How does Thomas's attitude—both before and after Jesus appears to him—add credibility to the resurrection?

7. How does Thomas's exclamation "My Lord and my God" (v. 28) provide a fitting climax to John's Gospel?

8. What can we learn from Jesus' encounter with Thomas about dealing with people who have doubts about Christianity?

9. Is believing that Jesus rose from the dead as important as believing that he died on the cross for our sins? Explain.

10. John tells us why he has written his Gospel in verses 30-31. Of all the "miraculous signs" John has included, which have been most convincing to you? Why?

13
A Walk with a Resurrected Man

John 21:1-25

Most of us find it easier to forgive than to forget. We may be ready to forgive someone who has hurt us deeply, but we have a hard time trusting that person again. Peter failed Jesus miserably. He promised to give up his life if necessary to protect Jesus but denied him a few hours later. Peter knew Jesus had forgiven him. But would Jesus still trust him? Could Jesus still use him to bring glory to God? Will Christ still use us after we've failed?

1. Describe how you feel when someone you have hurt refuses to forgive you.

2. Read John 21:1-14 What was the significance of Peter's decision to return to fishing (vv. 1-3)?

3. What was Jesus trying to show the disciples by allowing them to catch such a large number of fish (vv. 4-6; see Lk 5:4-11)?

4. When Peter hears that "It is the Lord," (vv. 7-8) he jumps into the water and begins swimming ahead of the boat. What does this reveal about Peter and his relationship with Jesus?

How would you have responded if you had denied the Lord only a few days earlier?

5. Read John 21:15-25. What subtle differences do you notice in Jesus' three questions and Peter's responses (vv. 15-17)?

What do you think is the significance of those differences?

6. What can we learn from this passage about the steps involved in restoring a Christian who has sinned?

7. Why do you think Jesus chose this particular time to predict the kind of death Peter would die (vv. 18-19)?

8. How does it help to know that you can still serve and glorify God no matter what your past failures have been?

9. What does Jesus' rebuke to Peter (v. 22) reveal about the danger of comparing ourselves with other Christians?

10. As you have studied through John's Gospel, what aspect of Jesus' character or ministry has impressed you most?

11. What responses have you made in your heart and life as a result of that deeper understanding?

Leader's Notes

Leading a Bible discussion can be an enjoyable and rewarding experience. But it can also be *scary*—especially if you've never done it before. If this is your feeling, you're in good company. When God asked Moses to lead the Israelites out of Egypt, he replied, "O Lord, please send someone else to do it!" (Ex 4:13).

When Solomon became king of Israel, he felt the task was far beyond his abilities. "I am only a little child and do not know how to carry out my duties. . . . Who is able to govern this great people of yours?" (1 Kings 3:7, 9).

When God called Jeremiah to be a prophet, he replied, "Ah, Sovereign LORD, . . . I do not know how to speak; I am only a child" (Jer 1:6).

The list goes on. The apostles were "unschooled, ordinary men" (Acts 4:13). Timothy was young, frail and frightened. Paul's "thorn in the flesh" made him feel weak. But God's response to all of his servants—including you—is essentially the same: "My grace is sufficient for you" (2 Cor 12:9). Relax. God helped these people in spite of their weaknesses, and he can help you in spite of your feelings of inadequacy.

There is another reason why you should feel encouraged. Leading a Bible discussion is not difficult if you follow certain guidelines. You don't need to be an expert on the Bible or a trained teacher. The suggestions listed below should enable you to effectively and enjoyably fulfill your role as leader.

Preparing to Lead

1. Ask God to help you understand and apply the passage to your own life. Unless this happens, you will not be prepared to lead others. Pray too for the various members of the group. Ask God to give you an enjoyable and profitable time together studying his Word.

2. As you begin each study, read and reread the assigned Bible passage to familiarize yourself with what the author is saying. In the case of book studies, you may want to read through the entire book prior to the first study. This will give you a helpful overview of its contents.

3. This study guide is based on the New International Version of the Bible. It will help you and the group if you use this translation as the basis for your study and discussion. Encourage others to use the NIV also, but allow them the freedom to use whatever translation they prefer.

4. Carefully work through each question in the study. Spend time in meditation and reflection as you formulate your answers.

5. Write your answers in the space provided in the study guide. This will help you to express your understanding of the passage clearly.

6. It might help you to have a Bible dictionary handy. Use it to look up any unfamiliar words, names or places. (For additional help on how to study a passage, see chapter five of *Leading Bible Discussions,* SU.)

7. Once you have finished your own study of the passage, familiarize yourself with the leader's notes for the study you are leading. These are designed to help you in several ways. First, they tell you the purpose the study guide author had in mind while writing the study. Take time to think through how the study questions work together to accomplish that purpose. Second, the notes provide you with additional background information or comments on some of the questions. This information can be useful if people have difficulty understanding or answering a question. Third, the leader's notes can alert you to potential problems you may encounter during the study.

8. If you wish to remind yourself of anything mentioned in the leader's notes, make a note to yourself below that question in the study.

Leading the Study
1. Begin the study on time. Unless you are leading an evangelistic Bible study, open with prayer, asking God to help you to understand and apply the passage.

2. Be sure that everyone in your group has a study guide. Encourage them to prepare beforehand for each discussion by working through the questions in the guide.

3. At the beginning of your first time together, explain that these studies are meant to be discussions not lectures. Encourage the members of the group to participate. However, do not put pressure on those who may be hesitant to speak during the first few sessions.

4. Read the introductory paragraph at the beginning of the discussion. This will orient the group to the passage being studied.

5. Read the passage aloud if you are studying one chapter or less. You may choose to do this yourself, or someone else may read if he or she has been asked to do so prior to the study. Longer passages may occasionally be read in parts at different times during the study. Some studies may cover several chapters. In such cases reading aloud would probably take too much time, so the group members should simply read the assigned passages prior to the study.

6. As you begin to ask the questions in the guide, keep several things in mind. First, the questions are designed to be used just as they are written. If you wish, you may simply read them aloud to the group. Or you may prefer to express them in your own words. However, unnecessary rewording of the questions is not recommended.

Second, the questions are intended to guide the group toward understanding and applying the *main idea* of the passage. The author of the guide has stated his or her view of this central idea in the *purpose* of the study in the leader's notes. You should try to understand how the passage expresses this idea and how the study questions work together to lead the group in that direction.

There may be times when it is appropriate to deviate from the study guide. For example, a question may have already been answered. If so, move on to the next question. Or someone may raise an important question not covered in the guide. Take time to discuss it! The important thing is to use discretion. There may be many routes you can travel to reach the goal of the study. But the easiest route is usually the one the author has suggested.

7. Avoid answering your own questions. If necessary, repeat or rephrase them until they are clearly understood. An eager group quickly becomes passive and silent if they think the leader will do most of the talking.

8. Don't be afraid of silence. People may need time to think about the question before formulating their answers.

9. Don't be content with just one answer. Ask, "What do the rest of you think?" or "Anything else?" until several people have given answers to the question.

10. Acknowledge all contributions. Try to be affirming whenever possible. Never reject an answer. If it is clearly wrong, ask, "Which verse led you to that conclusion?" or again, "What do the rest of you think?"

11. Don't expect every answer to be addressed to you, even though this will probably happen at first. As group members become more at ease, they will begin to truly interact with each other. This is one sign of a healthy discussion.

12. Don't be afraid of controversy. It can be very stimulating. If you don't resolve an issue completely, don't be frustrated. Move on and keep it in mind for later. A subsequent study may solve the problem.

13. Stick to the passage under consideration. It should be the source for answering the questions. Discourage the group from unnecessary cross-referencing. Likewise, stick to the subject and avoid going off on tangents.

14. Periodically summarize what the *group* has said about the passage. This helps to draw together the various ideas mentioned and gives continuity to the study. But don't preach.

15. Conclude your time together with conversational prayer. Be sure to ask God's help to apply those things which you learned in the study.

16. End on time.

Many more suggestions and helps are found in *Leading Bible Discussions* (SU). Reading and studying through that would be well worth your time.

Components of Small Groups

A healthy small group should do more than study the Bible. There are four components you should consider as you structure your time together.

Nurture. Being a part of a small group should be a nurturing and edifying experience. You should grow in your knowledge and love of God and each other. If we are to properly love God, we must know and keep his commandments (Jn 14:15). That is why Bible study should be a foundational part of your small group. But you can be nurtured by other things as well. You can memorize Scripture, read and discuss a book, or occasionally listen to a tape of a good speaker.

Community. Most people have a need for close friendships. Your small group can be an excellent place to cultivate such relationships. Allow time for informal interaction before and after the study. Have a time of sharing during the meeting. Do fun things together as a group, such as a potluck supper or a picnic. Have someone bring refreshments to the meeting. Be creative!

Worship. A portion of your time together can be spent in worship and prayer. Praise God together for who he is. Thank him for what he has done and is doing in your lives and in the world. Pray for each other's needs. Ask God to help you to apply what you have learned. Sing hymns together.

Mission. Many small groups decide to work together in some form of outreach. This can be a practical way of applying what you have learned. You can host a series of evangelistic discussions for your friends or neighbors. You can visit people at a home for the elderly. Help a widow with cleaning or repair jobs around her home. Such projects can have a transforming influence on your group.

For a detailed discussion of the nature and function of small groups, read *Small Group Leaders' Handbook* (Downers Grove, Ill.: InterVarsity Press) or *Good Things Come in Small Groups* (SU).

Almost every statement I have made about the Gospel of John in the introduction to the study guide has been challenged by some New Testament scholar! I have written from the position held by most evangelical students of John's Gospel. As group leader, it might be helpful for you to read a conservative introduction to the Gospel. The standard work (both introduction and commentary) is by Leon Morris (*The Gospel According to John*, New International Commentaries on the New Testament [Grand Rapids, Mich.: Eerdmans, 1971]). It is a massive scholarly volume but is filled with insight and devotion to Christ.

Other sources are:

F. F. Bruce, *The Gospel of John* (Marshall Pickering, 1983).

Craig Blomberg, *The Historical Reliability of the Gospels* (InterVarsity Press, 1987).

One profitable way to introduce your group to John's Gospel might be to compare the four Gospels in regard to their authorship, audience, purpose and message. In that way you can emphasize John's unique contribution to our understanding of Jesus Christ. Any Bible handbook will give you help in putting together such a comparison.

Part 1. Jesus the Living Word of God. John 1—12.
Study 1. The Master & Five Who Followed. John 1:1-51.

Purpose: To introduce John's message about Jesus and to demonstrate the impact Jesus had in people's lives.

The first 18 verses of John's Gospel (often called the prologue) are not as much an introduction to the Gospel as they are a condensation of John's whole message.

John states the basic truths about Jesus that he wants to communicate to us and then uses the remainder of the book to prove what he says in the prologue.

Question 1. Every study begins with an "approach" question, which is meant to be asked before the passage is read. These questions are important for several reasons.

First, they help the group to warm up to each other. No matter how well a group may know each other, there is always a stiffness that needs to be overcome before people will begin to talk openly. A good question will break the ice.

Second, approach questions get people thinking along the lines of the topic of the study. Most people will have lots of different things going on in their minds (dinner, an important meeting coming up, how to get the car fixed) that will have nothing to do with the study. A creative question will get their attention and draw them into the discussion.

Third, approach questions can reveal where our thoughts or feelings need to be transformed by Scripture. That is why it is especially important not to read the passage before the approach question is asked. The passage will tend to color the honest reactions people would otherwise give because they are, of course, supposed to think the way the Bible does. Giving honest responses before they find out what the Bible says may help them see where their thoughts or attitudes need to be changed.

Question 2. By using the title *the Word* for Jesus, John was declaring that Jesus is the full expression of God to us. Just as we express our thoughts to others through words, God expressed himself to humanity in Jesus. A good parallel passage is Hebrews 1:1-2.

Question 3. The assertion in John 1:1 that "the Word was God" is challenged by some modern cults. Jehovah's Witnesses contend, for example, that because no definite article appears before the word *God* in the Greek text, this phrase should be translated "the Word was *a* god." No evangelical (or non-evangelical) Greek scholar agrees with that translation. The absence of the definite article stresses that Jesus was distinct from the Father but was fully God just the same. For further detail see Morris, *According to John,* pp. 76-78.

Question 8. Be sure to distinguish between John the Baptizer (the "John" of verses 15-34) and John the Apostle (the author of the book and the unnamed disciple in verses 35 and 40).

Study 2. Wine & a Whip. John 2:1-25.

Purpose: To confront the student with Jesus' power over creation and his authority as God's Christ.

Question 2. In Jesus' day the wedding feast for the family and friends of the bride and groom lasted between two and seven days. The groom's parents were responsible for feeding and caring for all the guests the entire time. If they ran out of food or wine during the feast, it was considered a very serious insult to the guests.

The Gospels never refer to Joseph as alive during Jesus' adult years. Probably Joseph died during Jesus' young adulthood. As the oldest son, Jesus had the responsibility of caring for Mary and helping her. It was natural, then, in this time of need for Mary to come to Jesus for help.

Question 4. Large water pots holding twenty to thirty gallons each were available at the feast for washing the feet of the guests as they arrived and for the subsequent ceremonial washing of hands required by Jewish tradition.

Question 7. The scene shifts in these verses from Cana to Jerusalem. Jesus went to Jerusalem to be with his family and his disciples for the celebration of Passover.

Passover was a great feast day commemorating Israel's deliverance from Egypt. Instead of leading the people into a time of praise and worship to God, however, the temple leaders used it as a moneymaking opportunity. Men selling animals were agents of the high priest, who sold "approved" sacrificial animals usually at three to five times their market value.

The priestly leaders had also determined that the annual temple tax could be paid only in Judean coinage. Jews from other parts of the empire who had come to worship in Jerusalem had to exchange their foreign coins for Judean coins at a very high profit for the money exchangers. The entire system was run as a monopoly by Annas, the high priest. In the popular language of the day, the temple courtyard was called "the Bazaar of Annas."

Jesus' actions in the temple meant lost profits for the priestly leaders. They now had a reason to hate Jesus. This was the first of two cleansings that Jesus carried out. This one came early in his ministry; the second came just a few days before his crucifixion (Mk 11:15-18; Mt 21:12-17).

Question 9. The disciples recognized Jesus' action as a fulfillment of prophecy (v. 17; see Ps 69:9).

Study 3. The New Birth. John 3:1-36.

Purpose: To grasp the meaning and significance of the new birth.

Question 4. Birth is just one of many New Testament pictures of what results when a person believes in Jesus Christ, but it is a powerful tool for helping people understand the complete transformation Jesus brings.

Question 5. Nicodemus was amazed at Jesus' insistence on a new birth because he put a great deal of trust in his first birth as a Jew. Yet the Old Testament Scriptures revealed that more was needed than physical birth into Israel. Men and women needed a new heart—a transformation before God (Jer 31:33; see also Rom 3:28-29).

As Jesus talked, Nicodemus began to recognize the importance of spiritual birth. His question, however, (v. 4) centered on how it could happen. Jesus responded by showing Nicodemus that the means of this new birth are not physical but spiritual. In order to receive this new birth, a person must be born not only of "water" or "flesh"—that is, born physically—but also of the Spirit. Only the Spirit of God can bring life to the human spirit. (The question of what Jesus meant by the phrase *born of water* has been widely debated by commentators and theologians. I have interpreted *water* to be parallel to *flesh,* which refers to natural birth.)

Question 10. You may want to have each person in the group share his or her answer to this question rather than to single out the suspected or known non-Christians. At some point during your study of John, you may want to talk privately with those who are unclear about the gospel or their commitment to Christ.

Question 14. This is a good place to emphasize the importance of following Christ in obedience (John the Baptist) as the direct result of being born again (Nicodemus). This is not to open the door to a long debate on "Lordship salvation" but both aspects of the Christian walk are discussed in chapter 3— that is, the new birth and new life under the lordship of Christ.

Study 4. Soul & Body—Saving & Healing. John 4:1-54.

Purpose: To equip us to minister effectively to people that God brings into our lives every day.

Question 2. Jewish hatred of Samaritans had deep historical and religious roots. Seven hundred and fifty years before Jesus' day, the Assyrians invaded the northern section of Israel and deported the people living there. They left only a few poor Jews in the land. Then the Assyrians imported other con-quered people and settled them in the former Jewish territory. The pagan gentile population intermarried with the Jewish people and produced a mixed racial group called the Samaritans. The orthodox Jews in southern Palestine looked at the Samaritans as a corrupt race and took great pains to remain separate from them. It was the accepted custom that Jews and Samar-itans would not drink from the same vessel.

Question 3. By asking for water, Jesus was deliberately crossing three cultural barriers. The first barrier was sexual—he talked to a woman. Jewish men were advised never to talk to any woman in public. The second barrier was moral— the woman was living in an immoral situation with a man to whom she was not married (v. 18). The third barrier was racial—the woman was a Samaritan. Jesus was willing to cross these barriers in order to reach a woman who needed to believe in him.

Question 4. *Living water* normally referred to running water, such as would be found in a river or stream. It was greatly preferred over still water, especially for ritual purification.

Question 6. The proper place to worship was another issue that separated Jews and Samaritans. Because the Jews in Jerusalem refused to let the Samaritans worship at the temple in Jerusalem, the Samaritans built their own temple on Mount Gerizim ("this mountain" in v. 20). The Jews promptly tore down the rival, apostate temple, but worship on Mount Gerizim continued. The hatred between Jews and Samaritans would be resolved only in God's new society—the church (see Acts 8:14-17).

Question 11. When Jesus told his disciples, "Open your eyes and look at the fields! They are ripe for harvest" (v. 35), he may have been pointing to the approaching crowd of Samaritans (vv. 39-40).

Study 5. Deity on Trial. John 5:1-47.

Purpose: To understand that those who reject Jesus as the Son of God do so because of their deliberate denial of convincing evidence.

In the first four chapters of John's Gospel, the people tended to respond to Jesus in belief. Beginning in chapter 5, however, a significant change takes place in their attitude toward him. Now his miracles no longer produce belief; they generate controversy. Men and women become hardened in their unbelief. This is seen particularly among the Jewish leaders of Jesus' day. Jesus challenged their rigid traditions and their burdensome legalist rules, and it got him in a lot of trouble.

Question 2. Some manuscripts of the New Testament include a section between verses 3 and 5 about the "moving of the waters" in the pool of Bethesda. (See footnote in the New International Version.) It is generally agreed that these verses were not part of the original text of John's Gospel, but they do reflect some of the superstition that surrounded the pool. The people believed that when the water in the pool moved it was because an angel was stirring it. They also believed that whoever stepped in the water first after it moved would be healed. The paralyzed man was bitter because no one would help him get to the water first. Someone always beat him to it. In fact, the water may have been moved by the periodic bubbling of an underground spring (Morris, *According to John,* p. 302).

Question 9. Encourage discussion about the validity and weight of the testimony of each "witness." Consider why Jesus singled out these particular witnesses.

Question 10. The Pharisees who challenged Jesus were particularly proud of their knowledge of the minutest detail of Scripture and their strict adherance to the Law of Moses. Jesus uses the things they boasted in to bring condemnation on them. These religious leaders has missed the whole point of God's truth!

Study 6. Jesus, the Bread of life. John 6:1-71.

Purpose: To awaken in us a new awareness of Jesus' ability and willingness to meet our needs.

Question 2. This miracle is commonly referred to as "the feeding of the five thousand." John does say in verse 10 that "the men sat down, about five thousand of them." Matthew in his account says that the figure did not include women and children (Mt 14:21). Many evangelical scholars estimate the size of the crowd to have been around fifteen thousand.

Question 3. Bring out the way that Jesus used real life problems to build faith in his disciples. Apply that to the specific life settings of those in your group. How can we use life's problems to challenge those we are seeking to disciple (for example, children or new leaders)?

Question 10. Some Christians think Jesus' statement about "eating [his flesh" and "drinking [his] blood" refers to the communion service, the Lord's Supper. On the basis of this passage they believe that the bread (Jesus' body) and the wine (Jesus' blood) of the Lord's Supper are required to be saved.

It seems better to understand Jesus' statement as a figure of speech, picturing belief in him as the source of spiritual life. Just as we eat bread and drink water to sustain physical life, so we receive Christ to sustain spiritual life.

Study 7. Confusion over Christ. John 7:1-52.

Purpose: To demonstrate how we can respond in a Christlike manner to those who attack our faith in Jesus.

Question 2. Jesus' "brothers" are actually his half-brothers. Jesus was born only of Mary; these brothers are later children of Mary and Joseph. Four brothers of Jesus are mentioned by name in the other Gospels—James, Joseph (Joses), Simon and Judas (Mt 13:55; Mk 6:3). Jesus also had at least two half-sisters (Mt 13:56; Mk 6:3). John specifically says that Jesus' brothers did not believe in him. Their comments to Jesus were made in sarcastic tones.

Most New Testament scholars believe that at least two brothers ultimately came to faith in Jesus. James became the leader of the Jerusalem church (Acts 15:6, 13) and was probably the author of the New Testament book of James

(Jas 1:1). Judas (not to be confused with Judas Iscariot) is usually identified as the author of the New Testament book of Jude (Jude 1).

Question 3. In some translations verses 6-10 give the impression that Jesus lied to his brothers. He said in verse 8: "I am not going up to this Feast" and then, in verse 10, he goes up in secret. Jesus, however, was not deceiving his brothers. The New International Version gives the correct interpretation of Jesus' statement by inserting the word *yet* in verse 8—"I am not yet going up to this Feast."

Question 5. The Feast of Tabernacles (or Booths) was one of the great religious celebrations in Israel. It took place in the fall of the year. For the eight days of the feast, the Jews lived in homemade shelters. They erected these on the roofs of their houses or on the slopes of the Mount of Olives. This national camp-out was a reminder of God's provision for Israel during their forty years of wandering in the wilderness under Moses. They had no permanent homes then—just tents. They trusted the Lord for water and food. The feast became a perpetual memorial to God's grace. It was a joyous feast centering on a lot of singing, dancing and rejoicing. There was also a tradition that the Messiah would come during the Feast of Tabernacles. In the middle of the feast (the fourth day) Jesus began to teach in the temple.

Question 7. The phrase "the Spirit had not been given" (v. 39) does not mean that the Spirit was absent. Jesus is referring to the time when the Holy Spirit would be given to his followers in power (see Acts 2). After that momentous day of Pentecost, believers would be aware of the Spirit's presence and ministry in their lives.

Study 8. Caught in Adultery. John 7:53—8:11.

Purpose: To show Jesus' compassion toward all of us who are guilty of sin.

In the New International Version, this section of John's Gospel (7:53—8:11) is separated from the verses preceding and following by solid lines. The verses are missing from most of our earliest Greek manuscripts of the Gospel of John. Most later manuscripts include the verses at this point in the text (although a few insert them at other places in John and a few make them part of Luke's Gospel). While it raises some textual problems, most evangelical scholars agree with Dr. F. F. Bruce, who calls it "a fragment of authentic gospel material not originally included in any of the four Gospels" (Bruce, *John,* p. 413). For a full discussion of the textual problems, see Morris, *According to John,* pp. 882-84.

Question 5. It is obvious that these men were using this woman to trap Jesus. If Jesus had agreed that she should be stoned, he would have immediately lost his reputation with the people as a man of grace. But if Jesus had set her free, he would have set himself in opposition to the Law of God.

Question 6. "There is no hint of why he wrote or what he wrote. . . . A not unlikely suggestion is that He wrote the words He later spoke. In other words His sentence was written as well as pronounced. . . . T. W. Manson is of this opinion. He says, 'the action of Jesus might be explained from the well-known practice in Roman criminal law, whereby the presiding judge first wrote down the sentence and then read it aloud from the written record . . . Jesus defeats the plotters by going through the form of pronouncing sentence in the best Roman style, but wording it so that it cannot be executed.' An ancient opinion is that Jesus wrote the sins of the accusers (cf. Job 13:26)" (Morris, *According to John,* p. 888 and note).

Study 9. Jesus, the Light of the World. John 8:12-59.

Purpose: To demonstrate how the claims of Jesus divide people according to the response of their hearts.

Question 2. The events of this chapter took place in the treasury area of the Temple in Jerusalem (v. 20). Jesus spoke at the end of Israel's Feast of Tabernacles (7:14). During that feast, large Menorahs (lampstands) were set up in the treasury area and were lit at night. It was against the background of these Menorahs that Jesus made his claim to be "the light of the world." The visual imagery was striking.

Question 7. It is not completely clear who speaks to Jesus in verse 33. Perhaps those who professed belief in Jesus suddenly find themselves challenging Jesus because their faith is shallow and untested. Their claims of belief were not supported by their content. Their statement that they as Jews "had never been slaves of anyone" was a major-league lie.

Study 10. A Blind Man Sees the Light. John 9:1-41.

Purpose: To encourage us to do the will of God, even when we risk opposition and misunderstanding.

Question 2. Jesus' answer to the disciples' question reveals that God takes full responsibility for the way he has made us. There are no mistakes in God's sovereign plan (see Ex 4:11 and Eph 1:11).

Jesus' remark that "neither this man nor his parents sinned" does not mean, of course, that they were sinless. He meant that the man's blindness was not the direct result of anyone's specific sin.

Question 5. There is no final answer to this question. Perhaps Jesus was using it as the means of awakening faith in the blind man's heart.

Study 11. The Shepherd & His Sheep. John 10:1-42.

Purpose: To provide us with strong assurance of Christ's love for us.

John 10:1-18 is a continuation of Jesus' answer to the Pharisees who challenged him in chapter 9. Jesus explains the character of the relationship between himself and those who genuinely believe in him.

The cultural background of this chapter is extremely significant for a proper understanding of its teaching. A first-century Palestinian shepherd raised sheep primarily for their wool. A shepherd lived with his sheep. He knew his sheep; he named his sheep. Every village had a communal sheepfold with only one door for the protection of the sheep at night. The shepherds took turns guarding the door. In the morning each shepherd would come to the sheepfold and "call" his sheep. He made his own unique sound, a clucking noise or a whistle. Only the shepherd's own sheep would recognize that sound and follow him.

Question 2. Jesus used the familiar picture of the shepherd and his sheep to convey a greater truth. John does not record any of Jesus' parables, which were so characteristic of Jesus' teaching ministry, but John does record some of the allegories that Jesus used. Another example is the allegory of the vine and the branches in chapter 15. In an allegory a common experience or object is used to convey spiritual truth. Jesus used the allegory of the sheepfold to picture our salvation and the intimacy of our relationship to the Savior.

Question 7. Between verses 21-22 of John 10, there is a time change. The events recorded in John 7:1—10:21 all occur within a few days during and after the Jewish Feast of Tabernacles. That feast was held in mid-October. In verse 22 of John 10 the scene shifts to the Feast of Dedication (Hanukkah). That feast was observed at the end of December. So between verses 21 and verse 22 ten weeks have passed in silence as far as John's record is concerned, but Jesus' message is on the same theme. He continues to talk about his sheep and about who he is in relation to the sheep.

Question 10. Jesus' argument can be explained like this:

a. In the Scriptures God says to some men, "You are gods." The reference is to Psalm 82:6, where God refers to his representatives in Israel.

b. No one could dispute the fact that God did say that, because the Scriptures cannot be broken. They are the final authority.

c. If the Scriptures used the word *gods* to refer to persons who simply represented God, how much more appropriate was it for Jesus to call himself the Son of God, especially since he had given them abundant proof of his deity? They refused to believe.

Study 12. Resurrection & Life. John 11:1-57.
Purpose: To be encouraged by Jesus' ultimate victory over death and his power to bring glory out of apparent tragedy.
Question 10. Careful distinction should be made between the reviving of Lazarus and the resurrection of Jesus. Lazarus was revived to the same kind of life he had lived before. Lazarus eventually died again. Jesus was resurrected to a new kind of life, never to die again.

Study 13. The King's Last Acts. John 12:1-50.
Purpose: To show us the value of seeking God's will and God's glory even if it means dying to our own desires and goals.
Question 2. The three Gospel writers who record Mary's anointing of Jesus (Matthew, Mark, and John) tell us that the perfume was very costly.

Ointments and perfumes like nard were imported from India and Arabia and were often purchased as investments. Judas accurately calculated the value of Mary's gift as equal to one year's wages. This pound of nard (or spikenard) may have been Mary's inheritance from her parents. But in comparison to her gratitude for raising Lazarus and her love for Jesus, her gift represented a very small sacrifice. Anointing was an act of worship and an expression of complete devotion.

Part 2. Jesus, the Living Way to God. John 13—21.
Study 1. The Son as a Slave. John 13:1-17.
Purpose: To impress us with Jesus' example of loving servanthood and to motivate us to display the same spirit.
Question 2. The famous portrayals of the Last Supper by artists are almost all incorrect. Jesus and his disciples were not sitting on chairs at a table. They were reclining on low couches arranged (most likely) in U around a low table. Jesus, as the guest of honor, reclined in the center position. John reclined on Jesus' right; Judas reclined on Jesus' left. Both men had places of honor next to Jesus.
Question 4. When people entered a house, it was customary to wash their feet. A water pot stood outside the door, and usually a slave was stationed there to perform the task. Often the job was given to a crippled or retarded slave who couldn't do anything else. If there was no slave at the door, one of the members of the group would wash the feet of the others out of courtesy. But on the day Jesus and his disciples came to the upper room, no one volunteered.
Question 8. Peter's unwillingness to have his feet washed was a response

that normally characterized unbelievers. But the other extreme ("wash me all over") missed the point too. Peter did not need to be rebathed (reborn); he needed cleansing from daily sin.

Study 2. The Betrayer & the Boaster. John 13:18-38.

Purpose: To teach us to look beyond surface appearance to genuine character when choosing our spiritual heroes.

Question 2. See note to question 2 in study 14 for details of the seating at the Last Supper.

Question 3. Judas' impending betrayal came as no surprise to Jesus (see Jn 6:66-71). Jesus knew Judas' intention, of course, and yet Jesus continued to minister to Judas in exactly the same way he ministered to his other disciples. No one knew from Jesus' attitude that Judas was the betrayer.

Question 4. Judas reclined to Jesus' left; John reclined on Jesus' right. John could easily lean back on Jesus and engage in intimate conversation that the other disciples may not have heard or understood. Jesus could also talk quietly with Judas without attracting undue attention. To dip bread in a dish and give it to another person at the table was an act of friendship. It is comparable to proposing a toast in our culture. Therefore, Jesus continued to reach out to Judas in love.

You may also want to discuss the statement in verse 27: "Satan entered into him." Judas is the only person described in Scripture as being personally indwelt by Satan. Consider why John would make this point.

Study 3. Comfort for a Troubled Heart. John 14:1-31.

Purpose: To understand and claim the comfort available to us in Christ and in his promises.

Question 6. This chapter contains the first of several sections in John's Gospel on the ministry of the Holy Spirit. If you are unfamiliar with the teaching of the New Testament on the Spirit and his work, it would be profitable to do some reading in a theological work that addresses this important area. Two suggestions are:

Charles Ryrie, *Basic Theology* (Wheaton, Ill.: Victor Books, 1986), pp. 341-90.

J. I. Packer, *Keep In Step With the Spirit* (InterVarsity Press, 1984), especially chapters 1 and 2.

Study 4. The Secret of Remaining. John 15:1-11.

Purpose: To challenge us to seek a deeper level of commitment to spiritual intimacy with the Lord Jesus.

Question 2. The vine is used in the Old Testament as a figure for the people of Israel as God's chosen people (see Ps 80:8-19). But the Psalmist also foresees the coming of a divine Redeemer—"the man at your right hand, the son of man you have raised up for yourself." Jesus was the *true* vine, the unfailing channel of God's grace and power.

Question 3. This is a good place in the study to insert the necessity of being a "branch" (that is, a Christian). No one shares in Christ's life unless there is a faith relationship to Christ.

Question 7. A number of views exist on what it means for a branch to be "cut off." One is that we lose our salvation if we are unfruitful. That view, however, seems to contradict some things that Jesus has said earlier in the Gospel about our security. A second view is that this is a reference to God's discipline brought to bear on an unproductive branch. The genuine believer does not become lost, but is reproved by God. A third view is that these branches were not genuine believers in the first place.

If a number of views are represented by members of your study, give time to a presentation of each view but be careful that this issue doesn't overshadow the rest of the biblical material. If everyone in the group seems to hold to one view, you may want to challenge that view to test the depth of conviction in the other members.

Study 5. The Cost of Friendship. John 15:12—16:4.

Purpose: To explore the personal relationship that Jesus desires to have with us and to use that relationship as a model for our other relationships.

Question 5. The hostility of the world is the price the believer pays for friendship with Christ. You need to draw the distinction between persecution for Christ's sake or persecution that comes because we do something personally offensive.

Study 6. Secrets of the Spirit. John 16:5-15.

Purpose: To realize the power of the Holy Spirit that is available to us as we face the struggles and problems of life.

Question 2. The Counselor mentioned in verse 7 is obviously the Holy Spirit (see 15:26; 16:13-15).

Verse 5 seems to be a contradiction. Someone did ask Jesus where he was going. Back in John 13:36, Peter said, "Lord, where are you going?" However, Peter was not concerned about Jesus' destination but about being parted from him. Instead of rejoicing because Jesus was going to the Father, he was sorrowful about being left alone.

Question 4. The Spirit's work toward the world is to "convict" the world of some important things. The word translated "convict" means to present evidence so as to convince. Those who hear the gospel are convinced by the Holy Spirit of certain facts about themselves and about Jesus. Even those who reject the gospel are convinced of its truth. Their rejection is a matter of the will. They deliberately choose to reject what they have been convinced is true.

Study 7. A Dying Leader's Last Command. John 16:16-33.

Purpose: To equip us to handle crisis situations for which we have no explanation or answers.

This section is especially conducive to open sharing of struggles, fears and failures. You may not have answers to the problems that emerge. The focus of the study is that, even in the times of greatest darkness and confusion, we have not been abandoned. We can still cling to the Father's love and the Spirit's presence. It might be profitable to end the study with specific prayer for the people and the needs in the group.

Study 8. The Master's Final Prayer. John 17:1-26.

Purpose: To reveal the concerns of Jesus' heart as he faced the cross and to see how those concerns should be our concerns as his followers.

Question 7. The word *sanctify* means to set apart. In Scripture it has a double thrust—to be set apart from sin and to be set apart for God's use. Explore those themes in your discussion.

Question 8-9. The tendency is to read organizational unity into Jesus' prayer instead of organic unity. It might be profitable to review the "unity" pictures Jesus has already used: one flock (Jn 10); Jesus as the vine (Jn 15) and so on.

Study 9. "Jesus, You're under Arrest!" John 18:1-27.

Purpose: To show Jesus' sovereign control and calm confidence in a time of trial, and to give us assurance in our difficulties.

Question 3. Jesus spoke a simple word of response: "I am." That was the name the Lord spoke to Moses from the burning bush in Exodus 3:14. Jesus attributed to himself the personal name of Jehovah, the Lord God!

Question 4. Jesus asked the soldiers to name the person they were seeking in order to protect his disciples. If they wanted only Jesus, the other men should be allowed to go free. Jesus knew that their faith was too weak to withstand this test, so he provided a way of escape for them.

Question 8. It may be helpful to outline the main events of Jesus' trials in sequence. A harmony of the Gospels or a study of the life of Christ should provide you with those details.

Two men are called "the high priest" in John 18—Caiaphas in verse 12 and Annas in verse 19. Annas was the legitimate high priest of Israel under Jewish law. Some years earlier, however, the Roman authorities decided to sell the office to the highest bidder. Annas proceeded to buy the position for a whole succession of men. Caiaphas, the high priest that year, was Annas's son-in-law. Because Annas was the real power behind the office, the Jewish leaders took Jesus to Annas first.

The other disciple mentioned in verse 15 has generally been identified as John, the author of this Gospel. John may have been from a priestly family and would, therefore, have been known to the high priest.

Study 10. Pilate on Trial. John 18:28—19:16.
Purpose: To demonstrate that, even though Jesus was crucified unjustly, he willingly submitted to death for our sins.

Question 2. Pontius Pilate was a Roman career bureaucrat about the same age as Jesus. His official title was Procurator of Judea. He came to Judea in A.D. 26, hoping that he would soon be promoted to a more civilized section of the empire. From the moment he arrived in Judea, however, everything went wrong. After two or three major political blunders, Pilate found himself at the mercy of the Jewish leaders. They knew that enough pressure would make Pilate do whatever they asked.

Jesus' final religious trial had been held in the temple area before the Sanhedrin, the Jewish supreme court. Right next to the temple was the Roman fortress of Antonia. The Roman army was stationed there and Pilate, the governor, lived there. So it required just a very short walk to bring Jesus to the civil authority for final condemnation.

Study 11. Obedient to Death. John 19:17-42.
Purpose: To grasp the incredible price Jesus paid for our redemption from sin.

Question 2. A fascinating article on the crucifixion of Jesus was published in 1986 by a medical doctor, a pastor and a graphic artist. If you wish to obtain a copy for your own research or for the group, the article is entitled "On the Physical Death of Jesus Christ" by William D. Edwards, Wesley Gabel and Floyd Hosmer, *The Journal of the American Medical Association* 255 (March 21, 1986):1455-63.

Question 7. John had to verify Jesus' actual death in order to substantiate a genuine resurrection in chapter 20. Every witness affirmed that Jesus was dead—John himself (v. 26), the executioners and Jesus' friends who take his body away.

The legs of the victim were broken in order to speed his death. Survival on the cross required the victim to push up with his legs so that his lungs could fill with air. Hanging from his hands produced paralysis in the diaphragm. Only the constant and painful up-and-down movement allowed the man to live. When his legs were broken, he could no longer push up and, as a result, died in a few minutes. A victim of crucifixion did not die from loss of blood, but from suffocation.

The blood and water that flowed from the spear wound in Jesus' side (v. 34) was another evidence of his death. The blood in the heart had already separated. The heavier red blood cells had separated from the plasma, the clear liquid John called *water*. John records this observation as another proof that Jesus actually died. Modern theories that Jesus swooned or fainted on the cross and later revived have no support in the facts recorded for us by eye-witnesses.

Study 12. The Son Is Up! John 20:1-31.
Purpose: To affirm the reality of the resurrection of Jesus, and to show how we can respond to people who doubt or disbelieve.

Question 3. The position of the burial wrappings (vv. 6-7) is a significant piece of evidence. Jewish burial practice involved wrapping the washed body in strips of linen from the shoulders to the toes. As the wrapping was done, a mixture of gummy spices was spread on the cloth to hold the binding and to cover the stench of decay. A large square of linen cloth was wrapped over the head and face and was tied under the jaw.

When Peter and John entered the tomb, they saw the linen burial cocoon still in place, but the body was gone. The cloth that had been around Jesus' head was in its place by itself. The resurrection body of Jesus had passed through the burial wrappings, and they had collapsed in place.

Study 13. A Walk with a Resurrected Man. John 21:1-25.
Purpose: To demonstrate Christ's ability to use us for his glory, no matter what our past failures have been.

Question 5. It is not immediately apparent in most English translations but, in the Greek text of this passage, Jesus uses different words for "love." Jesus asks Peter twice, "Do you truly love me?" (vv. 15-16). In his question Jesus uses the verb *agapaō*. In his response "Yes, Lord you know that I love you," Peter uses the verb *phileō*. The third time Jesus asks the question, he too uses the verb *phileō*.

While a majority of scholars hold that these two verbs are essentially synonymous in this passage, a case can be made that the change is intentional and significant. Those who hold the change to be significant stress the uniquely Christian use of *agapaō*, "to choose to love and to commit oneself sacrificially to the person loved." *Phileō*, on the other hand, is generally used of love between friends and relatives; it stresses love based on relationship and emotional attachment.

The Living Bible and J. B. Phillips, as well as a marginal note in the New English Bible, suggest translations that reflect this difference. Peter responds, "Yes, Lord, you know that I am your friend." And finally Jesus asks, "Are you my friend?"

If we accept that the difference is significant, then it appears that, even though Peter's love has not become all that Christ wants it to be, Jesus is still willing to use Peter in ministry, saying, "Take care of my sheep."

Question 7. Perhaps Jesus began discussing death to keep Peter from being overly confident about his loyalty to Christ in the future. He also gave Peter assurance that even his death was under Christ's control.

We are never told in the Bible about Peter's death but several early Christian writers give us the details. Peter was arrested by order of the Roman emperor, Nero. When he was taken to be crucified, Peter asked to be crucified upside down. He did not consider himself worthy to die in the same manner as his Lord. His request was granted.

Douglas Connelly is a Christian writer and speaker who lives in Flint, Michigan.